For my mom, whose unwavering support
keeps me afloat in the stormiest of seas.

For Barry, Katie, Olivia, and Joyce—
My love runs deeper than the ocean.

—Deirdre

For my father,
who taught me the value
of adventure and travel.

—Carlos

Text Copyright © 2025 Deirdre Laide
Illustration Copyright © 2025 Carlos Vélez Aguilera
Design Copyright © 2025 Tilbury House Publishers
ISBN 9781668944882 (hardcover)

Library of Congress Cataloging-in-Publication Data has been filed
and is available at https://lccn.loc.gov/2025008541

Publisher expressly prohibits the use of this work in connection with the
development of any software program, including, without limitation, training a
machine learning or generative artificial intelligence (AI)system.

All rights reserved. No part of this book may be reproduced in
any manner without the express written consent of the publisher,
except in the case of brief excerpts in critical reviews and articles.
All inquiries should be addressed to:

TILBURY HOUSE
PUBLISHERS™

an imprint of
Cherry Lake Publishing Group
2395 South Huron Parkway, Suite 200
Ann Arbor, MI 48104
www.tilburyhouse.com

Printed in South Korea

10 9 8 7 6 5 4 3 2 1

SHIPWRECK

By Deirdre Laide

Art by Carlos Vélez Aguilera

TILBURY HOUSE PUBLISHERS

A vessel
floats on
flowing
waters,
glides on the ocean-wide,
cuts into the calm,
courses into crashing waves,
until . . .
it hits
a swirling storm,
　a rigid rock,
　　a silty sandbank,
　　　a mighty iceberg,
and becomes . . .

What will you discover?

A SHIPWRECK is the remains of a ship that has run aground or sunk in a body of water. There it will lie, abandoned, unless found by accident or quest.

Shipwrecks are waiting for curious explorers to discover their resting remains.

Will you find hidden histories?

There are over 3 million undiscovered shipwrecks in the world. Some shipwrecks are discovered accidentally, by curious divers and amateur explorers, while others are intentionally hunted and found by teams of professional adventurers, geologists, and marine scientists. They use advanced technology and expensive equipment such as sonar sensing, lasers, remote operated vehicles (ROVs), artificial intelligence, satellite mapping and, sometimes, good old-fashioned seafaring detective work. Around the world, there are so many shipwrecks to be discovered

Endurance

Trapped
by the frozen waters of Antarctica,
crushed
in a carpet of ice,
a ship
slowly
sank
ten thousand feet:
deep
deep
down
beneath the surface.

Planks
of strong oak wood
emblazoned
with an arched name
were found
preserved
in the freezing waters.

ENDURANCE

Do you see secrets from the past?

ENDURANCE was a three-masted ship that sailed from Plymouth, United Kingdom on an epic Antarctic expedition in 1914. Led by Sir Ernest Shackleton, with a crew of twenty-seven men (including one stowaway), eighteen dogs, and a cat fondly named Mrs. Chippy, they set off on their dangerous journey. In January 1915, the ship became trapped and crushed by ice before finally sinking, forcing Shackleton and his crew to embark on an astonishing escape from the Antarctic ice. Through teamwork, resilience, and strength, all crew survived. On March 5, 2022, the *Endurance* was found 9,869 feet deep in the ice-cold waters by the Endurance22 expedition, a team led by Dr. John Shears, a polar geographer, and Mensun Bound, a marine archaeologist. The sub-sea team, led by Nico Vincent, used hybrid Autonomous Underwater Vehicles (AUVs) to scan the sea floor. Due to cold temperatures and darkness, the *Endurance* had been preserved in excellent condition.

NUESTRA SEÑORA DE ATOCHA

Nuestra Señora de Atocha

Thrashed and tossed
in a howling hurricane,
laden with glittering gold,
silver, and
Colombian emeralds,
a ship was swallowed
by the stormy seas
near the Florida Keys.
Teeming with treasure chests,
it disappeared without a trace.

Determined,
a daring diver
and treasure hunter
uncovered
the precious haul,
once destined
for the King of Spain.

NUESTRA SEÑORA DE ATOCHA

Can you see precious treasures?

NUESTRA SEÑORA DE ATOCHA was a Spanish galleon laden with copper, silver, gold, Colombian emeralds, and other precious gems, bound for the King of Spain when it sank in a hurricane off the Florida Keys, United States in 1622.

Treasure hunter Mel Fisher and his crew found the famous shipwreck in 1985. The cargo's value was estimated at an amazing $400 million. Among other things, the treasure contained a collection of gold "money chains" long enough to hang past the waist, which were made to store and use gold at a time when the New World was not permitted to mint coins. Fisher wore one when he appeared on television. Some of the haul has been sold, while the rest is on display in the Mel Fisher Maritime Museum in Key West, Florida.

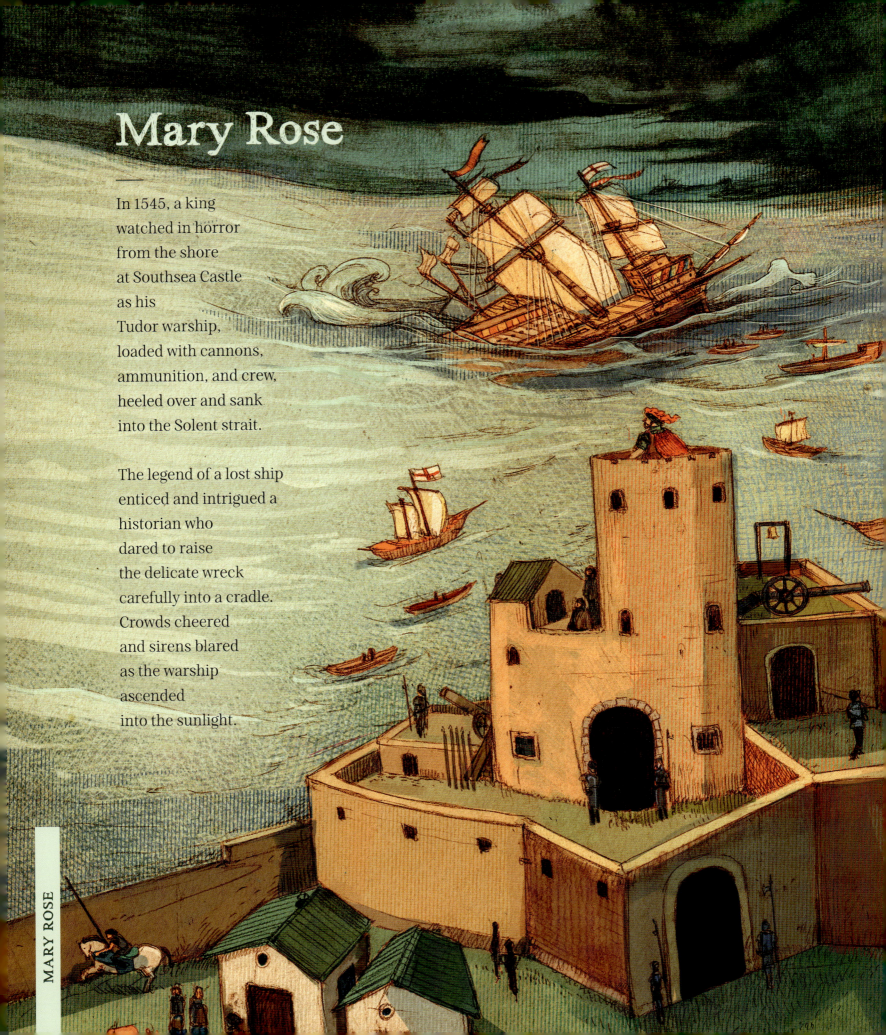

Mary Rose

In 1545, a king watched in horror from the shore at Southsea Castle as his Tudor warship, loaded with cannons, ammunition, and crew, heeled over and sank into the Solent strait.

The legend of a lost ship enticed and intrigued a historian who dared to raise the delicate wreck carefully into a cradle. Crowds cheered and sirens blared as the warship ascended into the sunlight.

Who dares to dive and discover?

The **MARY ROSE** was a Tudor warship built in Portsmouth, England for King Henry VIII's formidable Naval fleet. Fondly named after his sister, the ship set sail on July 19, 1545, to attack an invading French fleet seen gathering offshore. As the vessel entered the stretch of waters known as the Solent, it heeled over and quickly sank. The King had an unobstructed view from his castle as the disaster unfolded.

In 1836, fishermen's nets became snagged in the wreck and divers were sent to investigate. Years later, historian Alexander McKee felt compelled to officially locate the forgotten vessel. He trawled the Solent seabed with sonar scans until one day his team saw a strange shape. Sending down diver Percy Ackland to investigate, they found the *Mary Rose* on May 1, 1971. McKee was determined to preserve the historical legacy of the *Mary Rose*, and along with "*Mary Rose* Trust," they raised the delicate shipwreck above the sea for all to behold in 1982.

Sultana

As wild waters rose to treetops,
a mighty steamboat
met with swirling spring floods.
Crammed with parole prisoners
it turned
    and tilted
        on the Mississippi.
A boiler blasted,
exploding in a fury of fire.
Raging flames engulfed the boat.
A drifting inferno,
against the inky dark of night,
it sank
down
to the bottom of the riverbed.

Covered by layers
of silty sand
and mounds of mud,
the wreck
was buried
until an eager historian
plotted
and planned.

Searching a soybean field,
he found . . .

SULTANA

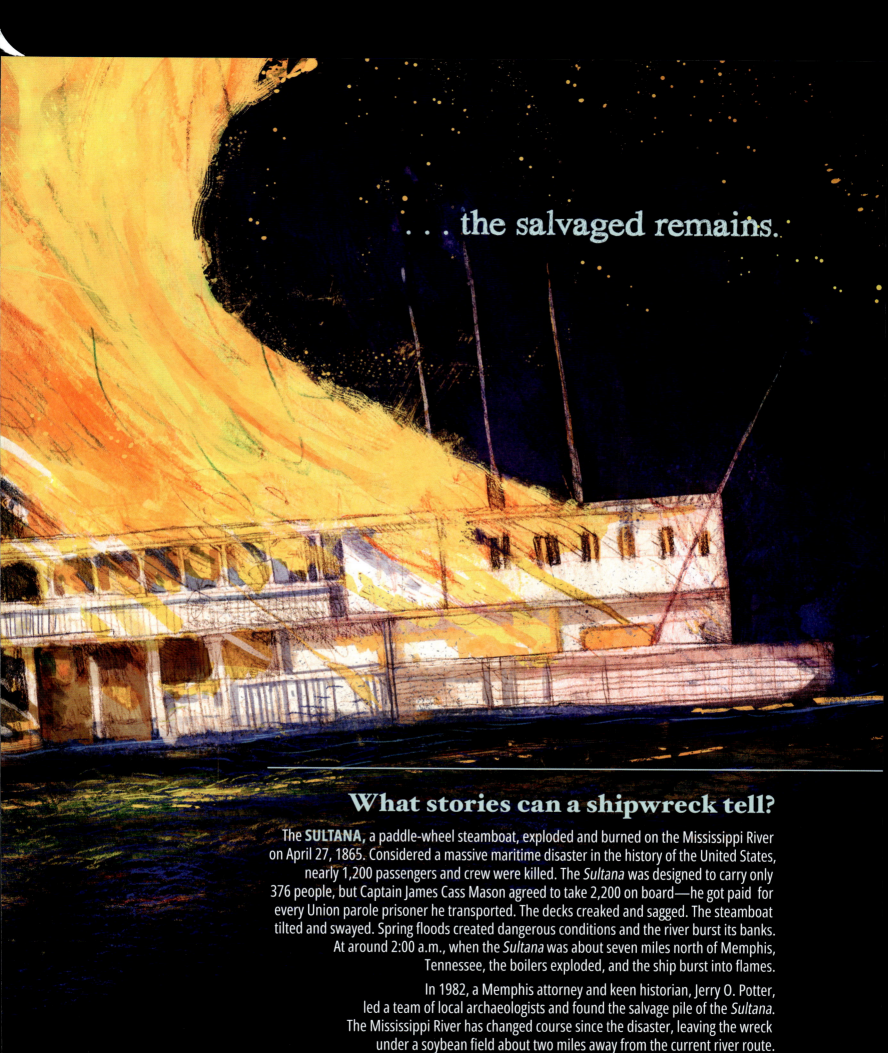

... the salvaged remains.

What stories can a shipwreck tell?

The **SULTANA**, a paddle-wheel steamboat, exploded and burned on the Mississippi River on April 27, 1865. Considered a massive maritime disaster in the history of the United States, nearly 1,200 passengers and crew were killed. The *Sultana* was designed to carry only 376 people, but Captain James Cass Mason agreed to take 2,200 on board—he got paid for every Union parole prisoner he transported. The decks creaked and sagged. The steamboat tilted and swayed. Spring floods created dangerous conditions and the river burst its banks. At around 2:00 a.m., when the *Sultana* was about seven miles north of Memphis, Tennessee, the boilers exploded, and the ship burst into flames.

In 1982, a Memphis attorney and keen historian, Jerry O. Potter, led a team of local archaeologists and found the salvage pile of the *Sultana*. The Mississippi River has changed course since the disaster, leaving the wreck under a soybean field about two miles away from the current river route.

LUSITANIA

Lusitania

Sprinting
across the sea,
an ocean greyhound
coursed
and cut
through
the Atlantic.
Hidden off the Irish coast,
a WWI submarine
lingered and lurked
beneath the surface,
armed and ready
to fire a deathly blow.
Peering from his periscope,
the U-boat captain
launched a torpedo
and watched it
swiftly streak and
BOOM
into the liner
with a mighty blast.

In 1935,
using a depth sounder,
a salvage steamer
scanned the South Celtic Sea
and found
the legendary
wartime wreck
of the sunken superliner.

What dangers lie beneath the surface?

The **RMS LUSITANIA** was famous for its speed and splendor. The luxurious liner was on its 202nd transatlantic voyage from New York to Liverpool as World War I tensions were intensifying between Germany, Britain, and their allies. Captain William Thomas Turner received a warning that he was entering warzone waters. On May 7, 1915, a German U-boat torpedoed the *Lusitania* off the coast of Ireland. Two huge explosions followed, sending a cloud of black dust and wreckage into the sky. Irish fishing vessels in the area rushed to the scene, attempting to save passengers and crew. In this wartime tragedy, 763 people survived and nearly 1,200 people lost their lives—128 of those were Americans. The disaster set off a chain of events that led to the United States entering World War I.

The wreck lay 11.5 miles off the coast of Kinsale, Ireland, in the South Celtic Sea until 1935 when it was discovered using some of the earliest diving equipment. Later, in 1993, under the direction of Robert Ballard—the oceanographer renowned for the Titanic discovery—a further in-depth survey was conducted of the ill-fated *Lusitania*.

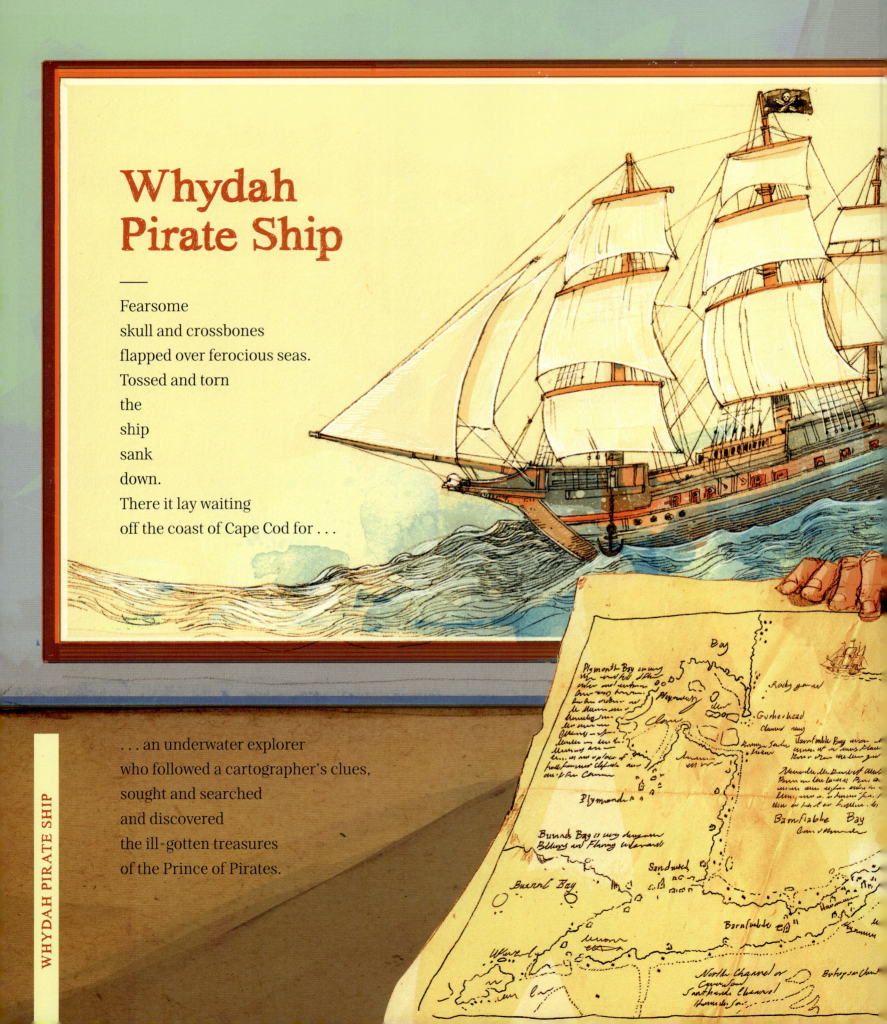

Whydah Pirate Ship

Fearsome
skull and crossbones
flapped over ferocious seas.
Tossed and torn
the
ship
sank
down.
There it lay waiting
off the coast of Cape Cod for . . .

. . . an underwater explorer
who followed a cartographer's clues,
sought and searched
and discovered
the ill-gotten treasures
of the Prince of Pirates.

WHYDAH PIRATE SHIP

Where does pirate treasure hide?

Originally commissioned in 1715 as a slave ship, the **WHYDAH GALLY** was captured by the notorious "Prince of Pirates," Samuel Bellamy, in 1717, off the Bahamas during the Golden Age of Piracy. Laden with a huge treasure trove, the ship was hit by a massive storm as it sailed along the coast of Cape Cod, Massachusetts, and smashed to pieces. Sinking, the treasure was swallowed by the sea.

In 1984, Barry Clifford, an underwater explorer and archaeologist, followed an 18th-century map marking the location and discovered the wreckage along with the teeming treasures of pirate Bellamy. At the Whydah Pirate Museum, Clifford has kept the hoard of artifacts, which includes tens of thousands of coins, cannons, gems, and everyday items used by the crew.

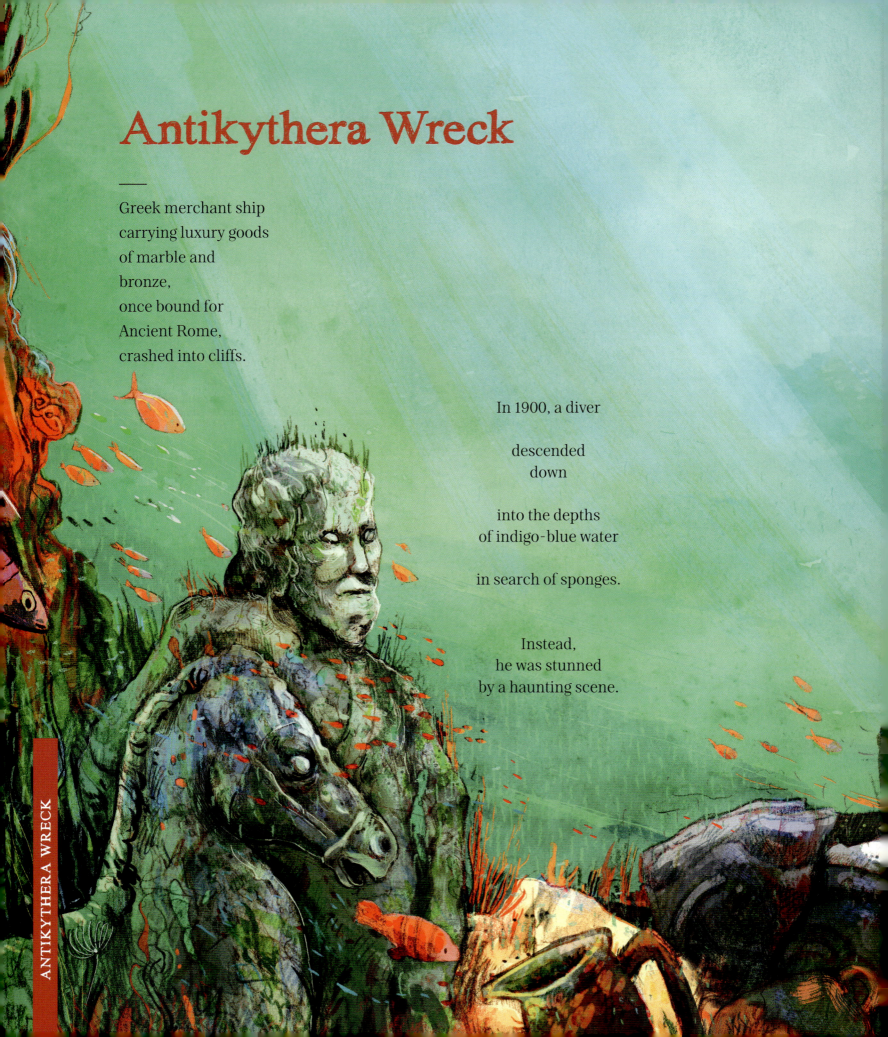

Antikythera Wreck

Greek merchant ship
carrying luxury goods
of marble and
bronze,
once bound for
Ancient Rome,
crashed into cliffs.

In 1900, a diver

descended
down

into the depths
of indigo-blue water

in search of sponges.

Instead,
he was stunned
by a haunting scene.

ANTIKYTHERA WRECK

What can these artifacts tell us about the past?

The **ANTIKYTHERA WRECK** yielded numerous statues, coins, and other artifacts dating as far back as the first century BCE. A strange metal disc was also discovered, now named the Antikythera mechanism. Using X-rays and CT scans, scientists found that the device was an elaborate construction of spinning gears that controlled dials tracking the sun, the moon, eclipses, and planets. It is considered the world's oldest analog computer.

In 1900, diver Elias Stadiatis was searching for sponges with basic diving equipment when he accidentally discovered the wreck along with its artifacts. At first glance, he got a terrible fright because the statues looked like real human bodies. A team of sponge divers worked tirelessly to excavate some of the priceless haul. In the 1970s, led by famous adventurer Jacques Cousteau, a team of divers recovered hundreds of objects in 27 days, including ceramic vessels, gemstones, fine glassware, and even human skeletal remains.

Titanic

Luxury liner
on a maiden voyage
accelerating
across
the Atlantic Ocean
crashed
into
an immense iceberg.

Freezing frosty waters
soaked and sucked—
the chambers
filling,
flooding,
and dragging . . .
the ship
down.

TITANIC

Now, a deep-sea graveyard
of scattered remains
it lies,
the resting relic of
the Ship of Dreams.

Will you find a lost ship?

The **RMS TITANIC** was a luxury steamship carrying passengers destined for New York City. On its maiden voyage, the ship hit a huge iceberg off the coast of Newfoundland. The *Titanic* sank in the early hours of April 15, 1912. More than 1,500 passengers and crew died in the cold waters of the icy North Atlantic.

Robert Ballard, famed explorer and marine oceanographer, was finishing a top-secret U.S. Navy investigation into the fates of two sunken nuclear submarines, when he joined with French scientist Jean-Louis Michel to search for the wreck of the *Titanic*. Down in the ocean's depths, Ballard's "Argo," a remote-controlled, deep-sea camera sled equipped with video cameras and lights, was towed behind a ship. The crew worked in shifts to keep watch around the clock. On September 1, 1985, they located the final resting place of the *Titanic*.

Vasa

Departing Stockholm harbor,
cheering crowds
watched in wonder,
mouths agape
they gasped
as a magnificent warship
opened its gunports and
fired
in a royal salute to the
King of Sweden.
A gust of wind filled the sails
and the top-heavy ship
heaved
and
heeled.
Sloshing, salty water
gushed
into open gunports
and it swiftly sank.

What do shipwrecks tell us about the past?

The **VASA** was considered the mightiest Swedish warship in the Baltic, but very briefly. Before it could leave Stockholm harbor on its maiden voyage, the ship sank in front of a large audience on August 10, 1628. Painted in bright colors, with several hundred carved sculptures, the *Vasa* was a floating work of art. A large lion jutted from the front, symbolizing King Gustav II Adolf's power and strength. As it set sail, a gust pushed the ship on its side and water poured in through the open gunports on the lower gundeck. The *Vasa* sank within minutes to the horror of all who watched.

VASA

A fuel engineer
searched the harbor
dragging a hook
up
and
down
until finally,
he snagged on
a small piece of black oak.
Deep
down
in the darkness
of freezing waters
teams worked together
to salvage
and save,
raise
and restore
the magnificent wreck.

In 1954, Anders Franzén, an engineer in the Swedish navy, started to search for the *Vasa* using a homemade coring device. He dragged the metal cylinder along the sea floor, pulling up samples. Finally, in 1956, he snagged on something special. It was a piece of black oak from the famous warship. Over several years, and after years of meticulous research and underwater explorations, a team of experts worked in the freezing waters to safely salvage the shipwreck and raise it up from its watery grave for all to see.

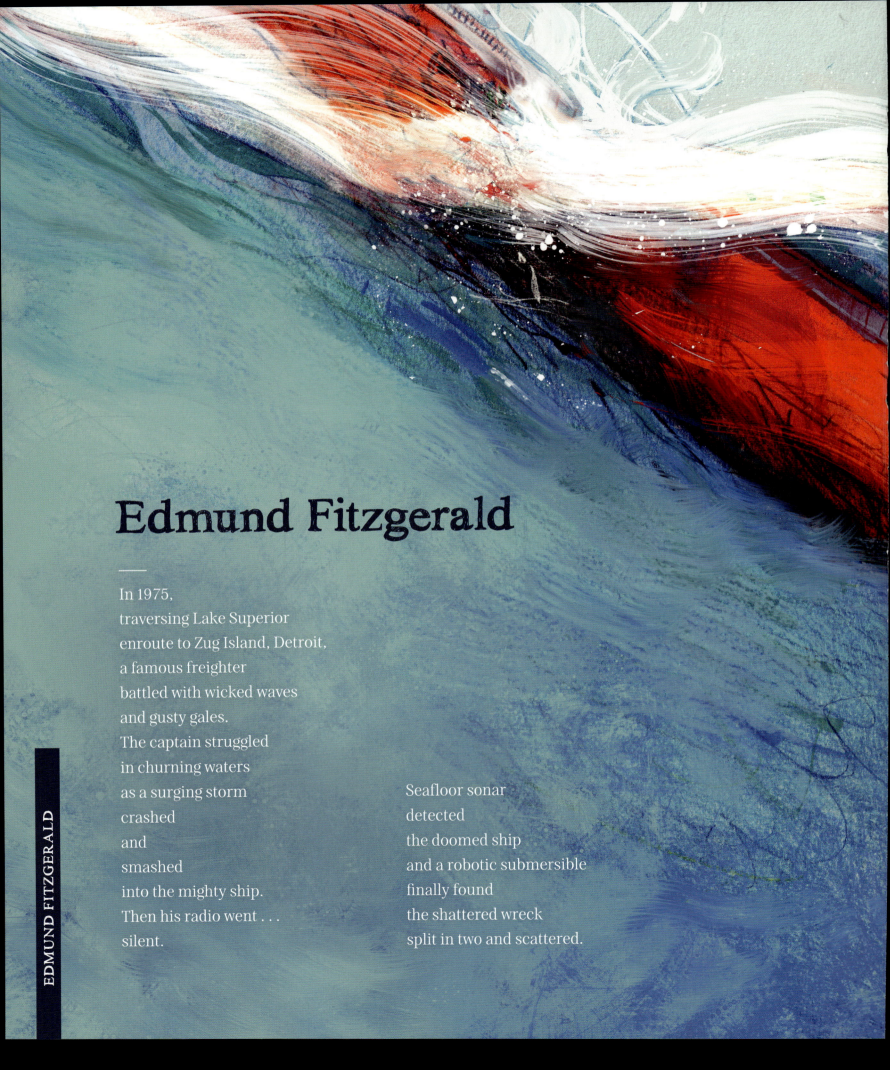

Edmund Fitzgerald

In 1975,
traversing Lake Superior
enroute to Zug Island, Detroit,
a famous freighter
battled with wicked waves
and gusty gales.
The captain struggled
in churning waters
as a surging storm
crashed
and
smashed
into the mighty ship.
Then his radio went . . .
silent.

Seafloor sonar
detected
the doomed ship
and a robotic submersible
finally found
the shattered wreck
split in two and scattered.

EDMUND FITZGERALD

Will you solve a mystery of the deep?

The **SS EDMUND FITZGERALD,** known fondly as "Mighty Fitz," was an American Great Lakes 729-foot ore freighter that became lost due to severe storms on November 10, 1975. The ship sank in Canadian waters, along with the entire crew of 29 men, on Lake Superior, near Whitefish Point, Michigan. The *Edmund Fitzgerald* is the largest ship to have sunk in the Great Lakes.

The storm subsided, and sonar technology detected two large objects underwater. In May 1976, a submersible robot located and photographed the mangled wreckage. Fitzgerald's 200-pound bronze bell was recovered on July 4, 1995, and sits in the Great Lakes Shipwreck Museum in Michigan. The exact cause of her sinking remains a mystery to this day. The tragedy inspired Gordon Lightfoot's famous folk ballad "The Wreck of the *Edmund Fitzgerald*."

"Superior, they said, never gives up her dead when the gales of November come early."

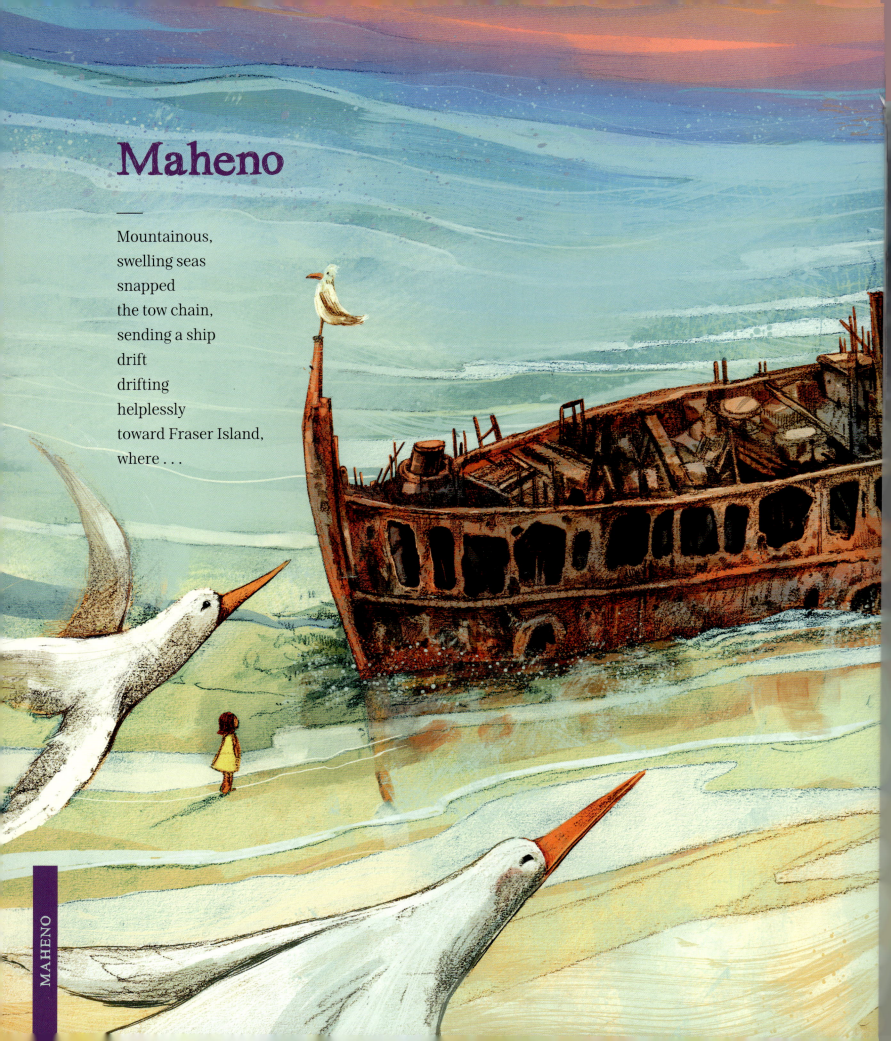

Maheno

Mountainous,
swelling seas
snapped
the tow chain,
sending a ship
drift
drifting
helplessly
toward Fraser Island,
where . . .

it settled
on the shifting sands
towering tall
into the skies,
a sleeping skeleton
breathing salty air
into a rusting ribcage.

Will you brave the wreckage?

The **SS MAHENO** was built in 1905 and was one of the first turbine-driven steamers. During World War I it became a hospital ship carrying and treating injured soldiers. It had two operating rooms, a laboratory, a steam disinfector, and even electric lifts. Known as "white ships," hospital ships had white hulls, green stripes, and red crosses. They helped injured people during the war, regardless of nationality, and did not interfere with combat.

No longer needed, in 1935 the *Maheno* was being towed to Japan for scrap when a cyclone hit, and the ship broke adrift. Landing on Fraser Island, Queensland, Australia, the wreckage has become a popular tourist attraction.

Oriskany

Colorful coral
and soft sponge
cloak the encrusted frame.
The sunken wreckage has become . . .
a rising reef home,
a plankton haven,
a rich habitat,
a helpful hideout, and . . .

a prowling predator's
hunting ground.

What sea creatures could you find in the deep sea?

The **USS ORISKANY** is the largest artificial reef in the world. It was originally built for the United States Navy after WWII. The Oriskany is 911 feet long and could hold up to 80 planes on board. Decommissioned in 1975, it was stripped and sunk in 2006 off the southern coast of Florida.

Accidental shipwrecks can cause terrible pollution due to oil and chemical spills. But sometimes ships are stripped of harmful materials and sunk on purpose to support marine life. Over time, the ocean transforms them into artificial reefs. New life flourishes with the growth of marine plants, sponges, and coral polyps. An abundance of small plankton comes to feed, followed by fish and hungry predators. Soon, the sunken ship becomes home to hundreds of sea creatures. The wreckage transforms from a relic to a reef.

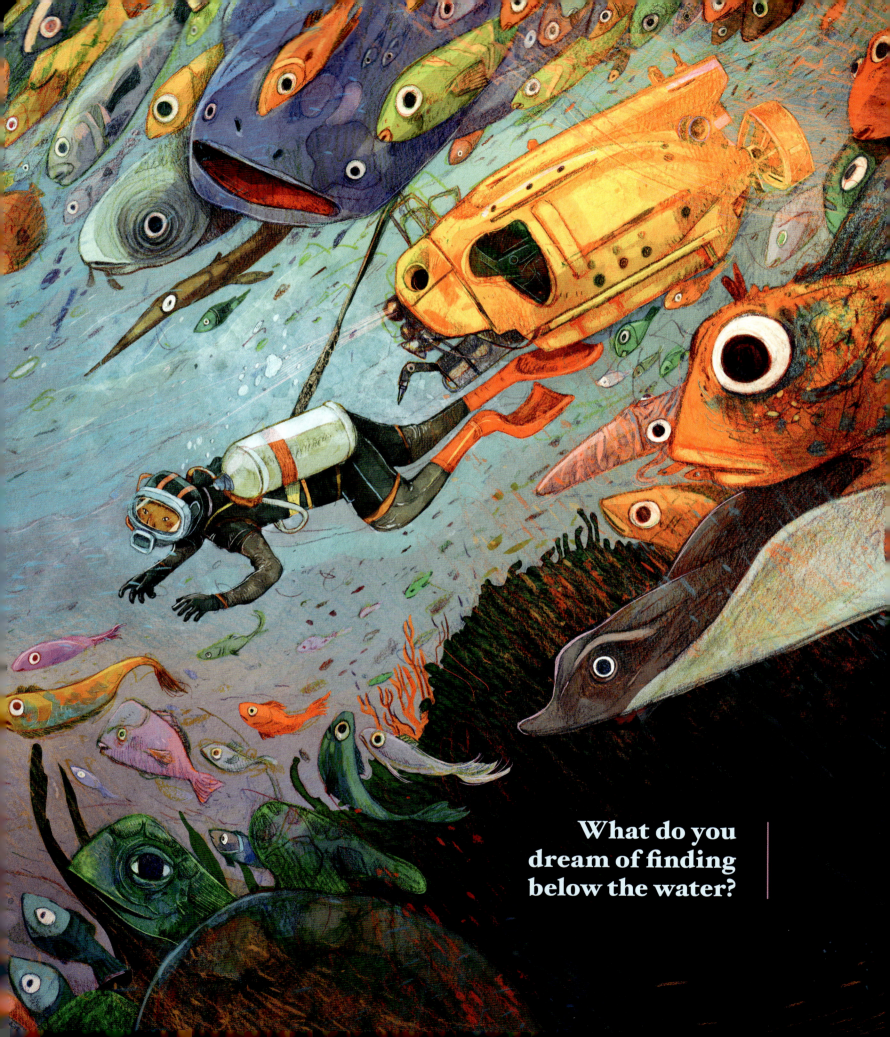

What do you dream of finding below the water?

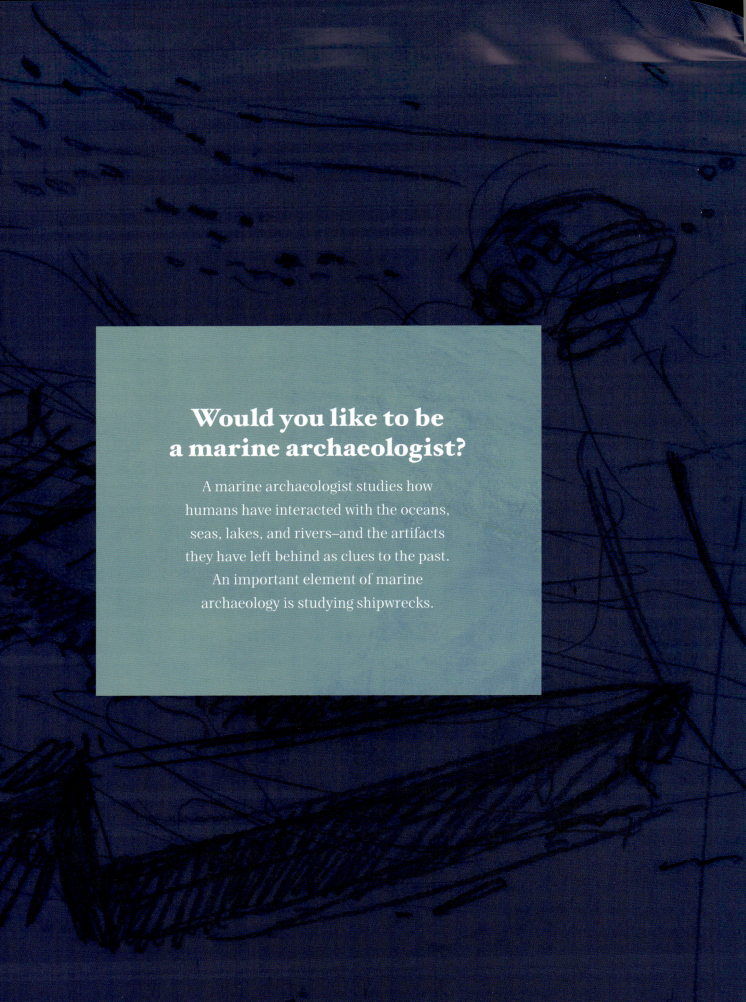

Would you like to be a marine archaeologist?

A marine archaeologist studies how humans have interacted with the oceans, seas, lakes, and rivers–and the artifacts they have left behind as clues to the past. An important element of marine archaeology is studying shipwrecks.

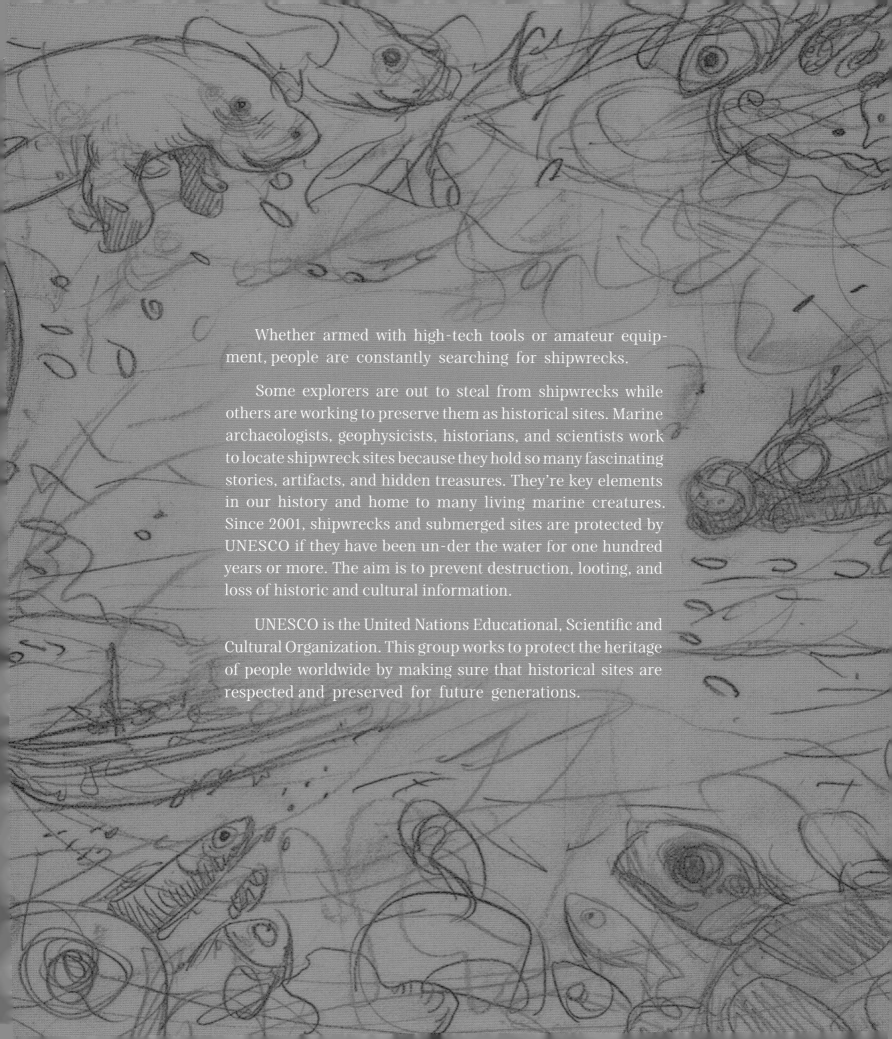

Whether armed with high-tech tools or amateur equipment, people are constantly searching for shipwrecks.

Some explorers are out to steal from shipwrecks while others are working to preserve them as historical sites. Marine archaeologists, geophysicists, historians, and scientists work to locate shipwreck sites because they hold so many fascinating stories, artifacts, and hidden treasures. They're key elements in our history and home to many living marine creatures. Since 2001, shipwrecks and submerged sites are protected by UNESCO if they have been un-der the water for one hundred years or more. The aim is to prevent destruction, looting, and loss of historic and cultural information.

UNESCO is the United Nations Educational, Scientific and Cultural Organization. This group works to protect the heritage of people worldwide by making sure that historical sites are respected and preserved for future generations.

A note from the author

I have always loved swimming in the ocean. Luckily, I live just a few minutes from the coast in County Kerry, Ireland. As a child, I would spend hours snorkeling in the sea and exploring rock pools. When living in Dubai, I became a certified diver and went on a dive to a shipwreck. I found it so fascinating. It felt like I had discovered a haunted, underwater house. As I swam around it, my heart pounded with excitement and a hint of fear. That image has stuck in my mind and inspired this book.

Tom Crean, a member of the 1914 *Endurance* expedition team to Antarctica with Ernest Shackleton, lived just twenty minutes from my hometown in Ireland. After his expedition, he returned to Ireland and opened a pub called The South Pole Inn. It still operates to this day and is adorned with memorabilia and photos. I've grown up with stories of his bravery and daring Antarctic expeditions.

—Deirdre Laide

Carlos Vélez Aguilera

was born and lives in Mexico City. He has been a professional illustrator for more than twelve years. He is a graduate of the National School of Plastic Arts of the National University Autonomous of Mexico. He has illustrated books for various publishers in Mexico and the United States and won a number of awards.

Deirdre Laide

is a teacher of young children, with a particular interest in social-emotional learning, nature, biodiversity, sustainability, and animal conservation. She adores writing fiction and lyrical non-fiction that create space for deeper discussions on important topics. This is her debut picture book. She lives in Ireland.